a walrus

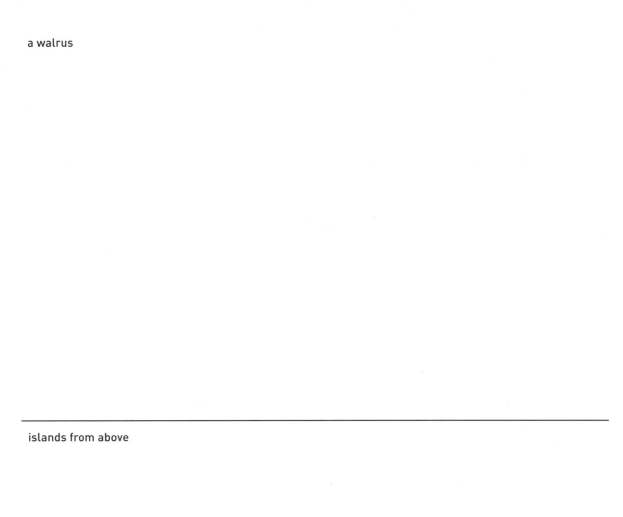

islands from above

a Grecian urn | a long highway

french fries and ketchup

a gas station sign

spots

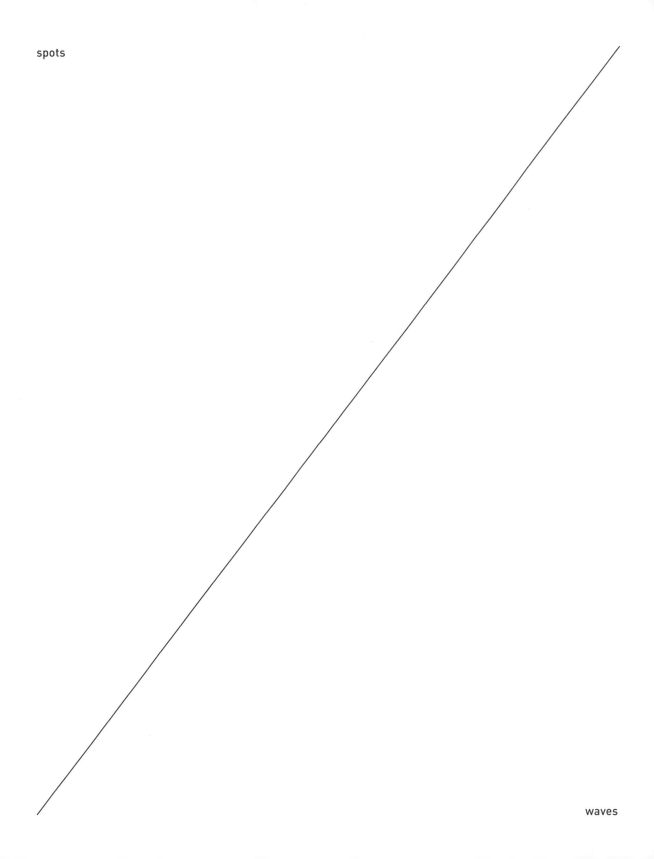

waves

a model airplane

a snowy field

a Persian rug

a broken pencil

falling from the sky

trees in winter

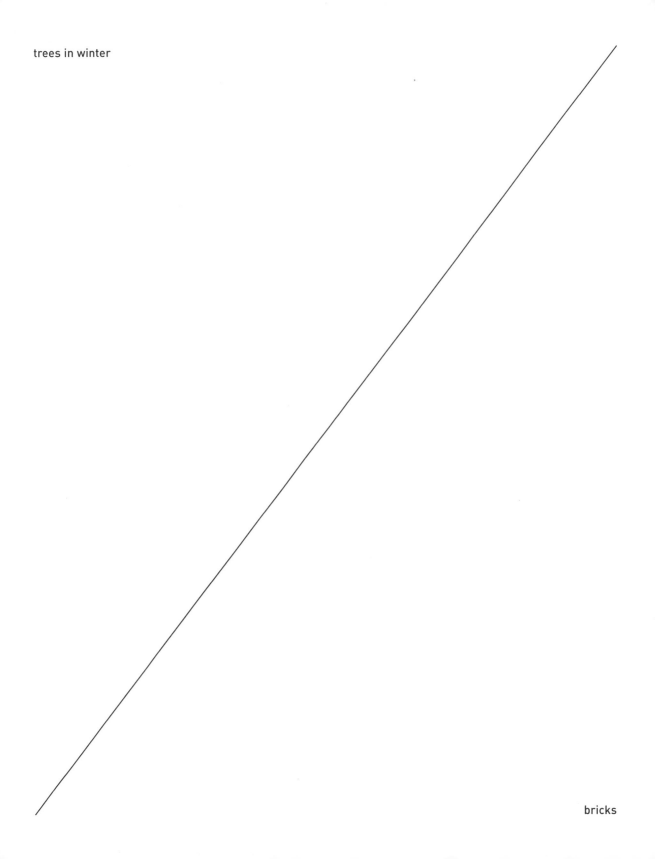

bricks

a caravan

---

soup ingredients

---

an empty beach

a green chair

a glass filled with ice

vines

grape soda

striped pajamas

a pile of laundry

a diamond mine

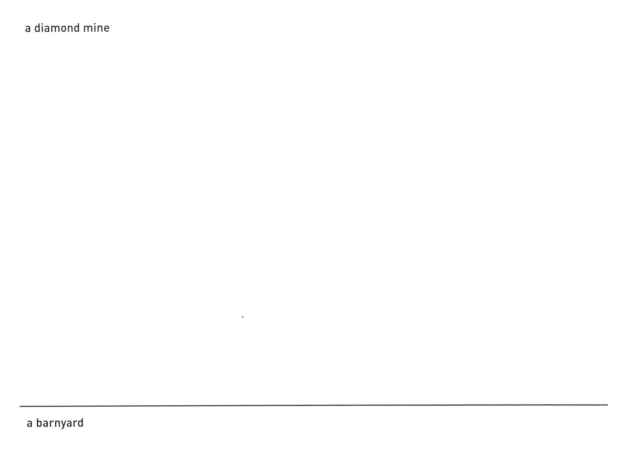

a barnyard

an atom

a brown paper bag

the number 101

a stamp

cozy

the Big Dipper

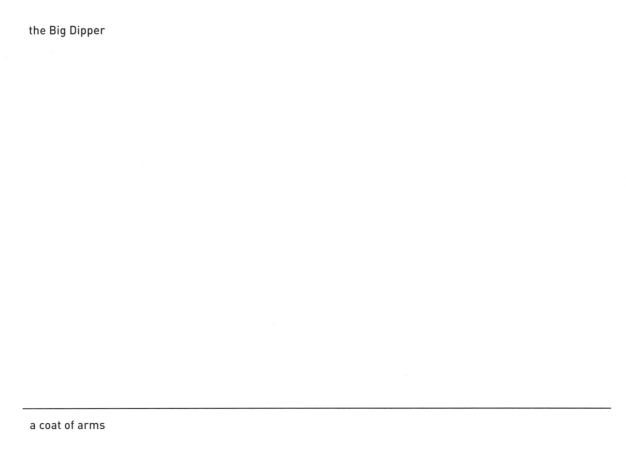

a coat of arms

arrows

migrating birds

a silhouette | the Mona Lisa

spilled wine

---

a china plate

a darkened movie theater

puppy love

a candlelit dinner

a tremor

a ray of sunlight

a detective | pylons

a condemned house

electrical wiring

an imaginary animal

rain through a window

something missing

strawberry jam

a mirror ball

an oily rag

a falling leaf

a sliced apple

a demolition derby

a radio tower

inside the refrigerator

a back alley

a spring thaw

storm clouds

calm

a sea captain

a school of jellyfish

a blue Monday

a clean desk

baby carrots

a peacock feather

toy boats

a long ribbon

orange cake

a staring contest

downhill | a nun

laughter

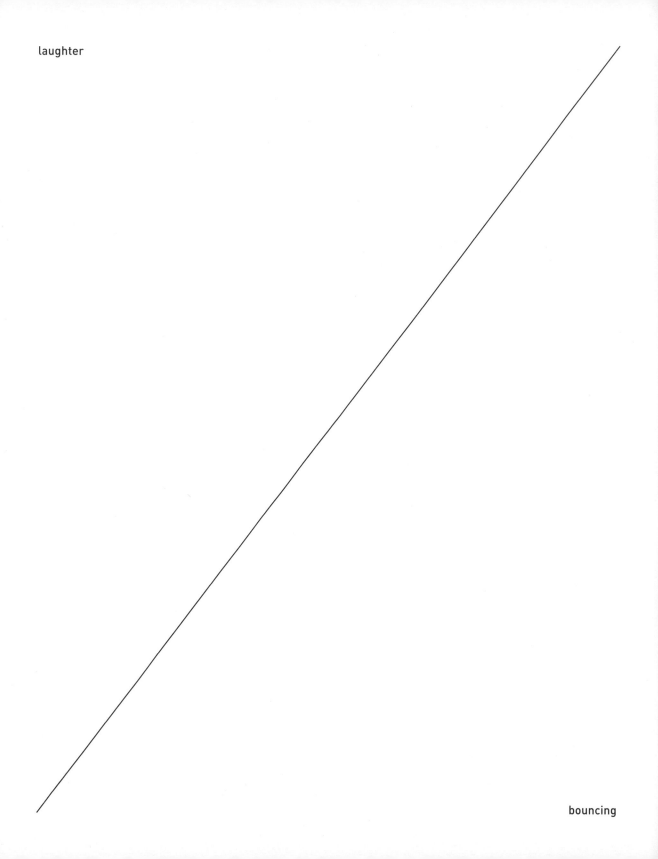

bouncing

moonlight on the water

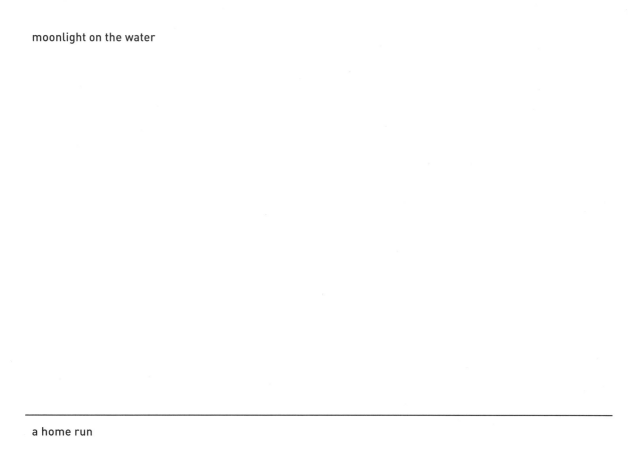

a home run

a department store window

an everything bagel

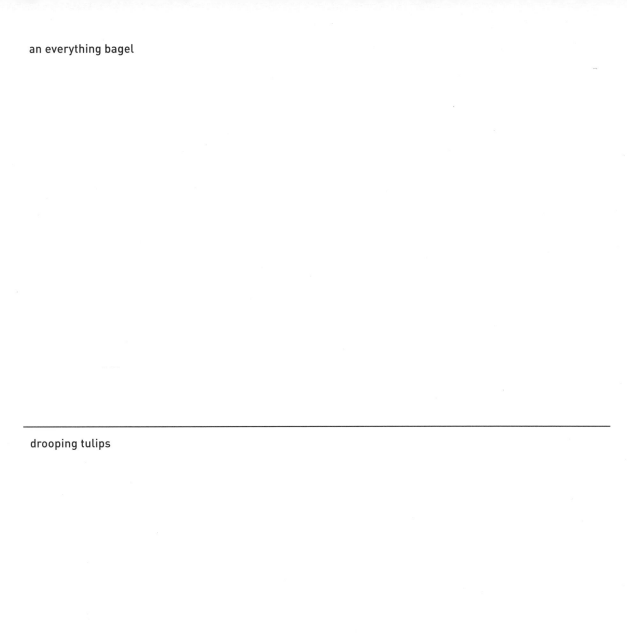

drooping tulips

a family portrait